WORLDS OF DIFFERENCE

Martin Palmer
Esther Bisset

WORLD WILDLIFE FUND

Blackie

WORLDS OF DIFFERENCE

BLACKIE & SON LTD.
Bishopbriggs Glasgow G64 2NZ
Furnival House   14-18 High Holborn   London WC1V 6BX

Educational edition	ISBN 0 216 91666 6
Trade edition (limp)	ISBN 0 216 91667 4
Trade edition (cased)	ISBN 0 216 91668 2

Picture Research: Alison Poustie
Illustrations: Jane Cunningham

Typeset in Great Britain by
The John Davidson Creative Group Ltd Glasgow
Printed in Great Britain by
Blantyre Printing & Binding Ltd, London and Glasgow

CONTENTS

ACKNOWLEDGMENTS

This project for the World Wildlife Fund was undertaken by the International Consultancy on Religion, Education and Culture. Our grateful thanks go to the large group of consultants and working party members who volunteered their ideas and insights throughout the project. In particular thanks are due to the following people: David Chapman, Rabbi Douglas Charing, Mike Edwards, Jack Hogbin, Ruby Khan, Daniel Mak, Peter Martin, Nigel Palmer, Mr and Mrs Panchmatia, Alison Poustie, Ranchor das, John Rawson, M A Salam, Mike Shackleton, Ralph Simons, Angela Smith and Barbara Tayler.

Many organizations assisted the project's work and advised on its content. We would like to extend our gratitude to the following individuals and organizations without whose help this work could never have been completed: the Astronomy Departments of Cambridge and Manchester Universities, Plymouth Polytechnic, and Lindy Brett; Roger Hutchins (BBC *Sunday* programme); Pauline Webb (BBC World Service); Clive Lawton (Board of British Deputies); Harry Stopes-Roe (British Humanist Association); Jay Southwick (Center for Congregational Education, USA); Tim Cooper (Christian Ecology Group); Rev Ian Corbett (Church of England Adult Education); Commonwealth Institute; John Baines and Stephen Stirling (Council for Environmental Education); Bob Kirby (Development Education Centre, Manchester); Dr Joseph Needham (East Asian History of Science Library); Hong Kong Tourist Office; the Editor, *Impact International* (Muslim News Magazine); E Prinja (Indian Association, Manchester); Mathoor Krishnamurti (Institute of Indian Culture); Rasa Mandala (ISKCON); Dr A A Mughram and Sheikh Solaiman (Islamic Cultural Centre); Dr M M Ahsan (Islamic Foundation); Werner Mayer (Jewish Museum, Manchester); Reuben Turner (Jewish National Fund); London Sevashram Sangha; Loret Lee (Manchester Chinese Cultural, Educational and Community Centre); Nikki van der Gaag (Minority Rights Group); Peter and Sylvia Dadd (Othona Community); Pictorial Charts Educational Trust; Ramakrishna Vedanṭa Centre; San Francisco Bi-lingual Program; Dr Hugh Baker, Paul Fox and Richard Tames (School of Oriental and African Studies); Andrew Crocker and Marcus Colchester (Survival International); USSR Embassy; Dr Dave Hicks (World Studies Project); Woonum and Jabanangka (Worldwind Co).

Finally, we would like to acknowledge our indebtedness to the many teachers, pupils, students and advisers who tested the materials for us. In particular our thanks go to Jane Gordon, Sale Girls' Grammar School; Chris Halliday; Sheila James and Phil Smith, St Agnes Church of England Primary School; Manchester Education Committee; Sandra Palmer; Tony Philips (Manchester Primary Multi-Culture/RE Projects Officer); Sue Phillips; Mr J Sayles and colleagues, Maltravers School; Alf Walker (BBC Education Officer); the staff and children of Wilbraham Road Junior School; Christine Winstanley (Manchester Secondary Schools RE Adviser); David Winston and colleagues, Egerton Primary School.

FOREWORD

Imagine how less meaningful our lives would be if we were not able to enjoy the beauty of nature - the presence of the birds and animals, the grandeur and mystery of the mountains, the awesome expanse and stillness of the ocean. In fact, it would be impossible for us to survive without them for they provide us with food and water.

But they share with us much more than that. I am sure many of you have a dog, cat or bird for a pet and how much it must mean to you. We love and value them because they provide us with comfort and companionship. Have you wondered what a beautiful place this world would be if everyone could treat all animals and life in the same manner. And realize the fact that, whether it is more complex groups like human beings or simpler groups such as animals, the feeling of pain and appreciation of happiness is common,- all want to live and do not wish to die.

As a Buddhist, I believe in the interdependence of all things, the interrelationship among the whole spectrum of plant and animal life, including the elements of nature which express as mountains, valleys, rivers, sky and sunshine. But you don't have to believe in a religion to realize the preciousness of life and the right of even the tiniest insect to exist.

Yet, as we look around, we witness needless cruelty to animals, defenceless as they are. Through the newspapers and television we come to know about the extinction of many forms of life, the degradation of the soil and plant life that have sustained us for so long.

No government or organization no matter how well its intention may be, can tackle the root of the problem without the awareness and participation of everyone in society. That is why the efforts of the World Wildlife Fund are so important and should be supported whole-heartedly by all of us.

The stories you will read in the following pages try to explain the way all forms of life are regarded by different people all over the world. Some of them may not sound factual but that is not the point. It is what we learn from the ideas behind them that matters.

Next time, when we are about to trample a plant, destroy a flower or kill a harmless insect, can we remember the message of some of these stories and in return for the gift and beauty nature has enriched our lives with, treat it with more gentleness and appreciation?

HIS HOLINESS
THE DALAI LAMA OF TIBET

August 8, 1984

PICTURE SOURCES

Michael Edwards and Alison Poustie: Aborigine maps, pages ii, 8, and bark painting of Barramundi fish, page 11 (all by arrangement with the Worldwind Company); children in classroom, page 4; Geomancis compass, page 15; Chinese landscape painting, page 17 (by arrangement with the Anglo-Chinese Educational Institute); Jewish food, page 38; Succot house, page 40 (by arrangement with the Jackson Row Reformed Synagogue, Manchester); tree planting, page 41.

Natural History Photographic Agency: fox eating squirrel by S Krasemann, page 1; fox cub by E A James, page 1; tiger by E Hanumantha Rao, page 34; white rhino grazing by Peter Johnson, page 34; community of African elephants by Anthony Bannister, page 46.

Woodmansterne Ltd: Earth from Apollo 17, page 2 (NASA); Wells Cathedral, page 18; stained glass window at York Minster showing the 5th day of creation, page 20; Western wall, Jerusalem, page 36.

J Allan Cash Ltd: Ayer's rock, page 6; sacred cows in Indian market, page 28; tree by the Dead Sea, page 39.

Australian Information Service, London: Olgas mountains in Australia, page 8; Aborigine in cave, page 9; Kookaburra bird, page 11.

Christine Osborne: Australian waterhole with flying foxes, page 10; Call to prayer, Pakistan, page 44; prayers at Eid, page 45.

David Chapman: South Putuo Temple, Xiamen, page 12; planting fields, Fujian province, page 15; landscape of Guilin, page 16.

Lu Tri Truyen, Chinese community centre, Manchester: P'an Ku holding the yin yang symbol, page 14.

Aberdeen University Library: Adam naming the animals from *Aberdeen Bestiary*, page 21.

Cath Cabarê: Harvest Festival, page 22.

John Goodman, R.S.P.C.A.: rescued baby badger, page 23.

India Government Tourist Office, London: Hindu temple, page 24; Indian fruit market, page 29.

Ann and Bury Peerless: Brahma, Vishnu and Shiva, page 26; Chola bronze of Dancing Shiva, page 27.

International Society for Krishna Consciousness: re-incarnation, page 27.

The Royal Observatory, Edinburgh: Orion, page 30.

Petur Simonardson: Surtsey volcanic island being born, page 32.

D Rodger, U.N.E.S.C.O.: UNESCO in session, page 35.

Turkish Tourist Office, London: Ishak Pasa palace, page 42; view of Uchisar, Turkey, page 47.

Marcus Colchester, Survival International: Amazonian forest village, page 48; Yanomamo men in boat, page 50; Sharmanists calling upon the animal spirits, page 51; Yanomamo children, page 52.

Keith and Liz Laidler, Oxford Scientific Films, Survival Anglia Ltd: Harpy eagle, page 53.

·Belief and the Environment·

The way that people look at the world around them depends on their background. Think about this question: What is a fox? To some people, it is a reddish-coloured animal which hunters chase on horseback. To animal lovers, the fox is a lively, rather rascally creature who has managed to live not just in the countryside, but also in the town. To the farmer, the fox is a pest which kills chickens. To someone who is against hunting, the fox is an innocent victim of human cruelty. To many storytellers in many lands, the fox is a clever and cunning character, as in the French story of Reynard the fox. To Hindus or Buddhists, the fox has a soul like their own, and may even be someone they knew before who has died and been reborn as a fox. To many Japanese people, the fox is a frightening sight, because they believe that evil spirits live in the bodies of foxes waiting to take over human beings.

So let us look at this question again: What is a fox? As you can see, the answers people give depends on what they believe. This is true of everything around us. We understand things because of what we believe. If you believe that hunting is wrong, then you will see animals like the fox, rabbit or tiger in one way. If you are a hunter, then you will see them in a very different way. If you like sausages, then you will see the pig as a source of food. If you are a vegetarian, then you will not. If you believe that the world is there to use as you want and when you want, then you are not going to care very much for it. If you believe that everything in the world is the same sort of being or soul as you, then you will be careful.

In this book we are going to look at the many ways that people see the world. We have chosen eight religions or belief systems. Each of them tells its own story about how and why the world, and everything that lives in it, began. From these stories we can then look and see what sort of world the believer sees, and how this leads him or her to behave in certain ways. This is why we have called this book *Worlds of Difference*. Quite simply, although we all live on the same planet, we actually see and feel different worlds. As an example, we all know that there are very powerful bombs called nuclear bombs. We know roughly what they can do. To some people, these bombs are peace-makers: because they are so powerful, no one will ever use them. They believe that this has made the world a safer place to live, because the big countries will not go to war. They are too scared of using the bomb. But other people see a very different world. They do not see the bombs as peace-makers. They see them as a terrible threat, which will probably wipe out the world one day. They see the big nations as great armies, which are getting bigger and bigger and will eventually go to war. Who is right? Well, that's up to you to decide. But from the same fact, the nuclear bomb, come two startlingly different views of the world — almost two different worlds.

The same is true of religious and other beliefs. Because of what we believe, we see different worlds. In this book, we are not going to ask you to tell us which world is the true one. To the believer, what they believe is true. The same is true for you. Whether you are a Christian, Hindu or Humanist, you believe certain things, and will probably be surprised to discover that not everyone agrees with you.

The stories and the believers

The stories have been taken from eight belief systems. Some talk about a god or gods. Others don't. But they all have one thing in common. Through words, they all try to describe the indescribable. They all use words to paint a picture. Some people believe that these stories are really how things happened. Others believe that they are pictures which try to help us to understand not just how we came to be, but why.

Just think about how you might tell a story about yourself. Imagine that you were walking to school one day, and a car suddenly crashed into a lamp-post beside you. You might say that the car appeared 'out of the blue'. The blue what? It's just a way of saying that you didn't see the car before. You were 'scared silly', and nearly 'jumped out of your skin'. You don't really mean that you are now daft and skinless! You are trying to help the person listening to feel what it was like.

The stories you are about to read are like this. They use words and descriptions to try to help you to enter someone else's world, to help you to see with someone else's eyes. So don't say, 'This isn't true'. Perhaps the facts may not be literally true, but to the storyteller the ideas behind the story are. It is these ideas which are the most important part of the stories.

Some of the stories are very old, and have been told for thousands of years. All the stories are special. They are very special to those who believe them, so we must treat them with respect. We are being invited into the very heart of people's beliefs. We should enjoy them, explore them, share them, argue over them. But we must remember how very precious they are to many people.

Because people have different ideas about the world and everything in it, they have different ways of life. The way people treat the world depends on how they look at the world. When you have looked at other people's ideas and beliefs in this book, we hope that you will start looking at your own. Perhaps you will have come across some ideas, stories, pictures, explanations and ways of life which you feel have something important to say to everyone. By sharing our ideas, our hopes and fears, perhaps we can all work together to care more for this world — or worlds.

Some useful information

There are different ways that this book could have been arranged. It could have started with the oldest stories, and ended with the newest. But since no one is sure whether certain stories are older than others, we decided it was fairest to put them in alphabetical order.

In the book, CE (Common Era) and BCE (Before the Common Era) have been used instead of BC and AD. BC and AD are Christian terms meaning 'Before Christ' and 'Year of our Lord', and can cause offence to people who are not Christians.

If there are any words in the book that you don't understand, look to see if they are in the Word List at the end of the book.

THE AUSTRALIAN · ABORIGINE WORLD

The Aborigines have lived on the vast island of Australia for at least forty thousand years. Their way of life — hunting wild animals and gathering grains and fruit — has made it possible for them to survive. In fact, they are one of the oldest surviving cultures in the world.

Each group has its own collection of stories and ceremonies. This is because each group's stories, including Dreamtime (creation) stories, tell of their own area of land. The stories are very sacred and many are secret, told only to members of the group.

There are many different groups. Before the white settlers came, from 1788 onwards, there were many more. Since then the history of the Aborigines is a terrible tale of cruelty, disease and death caused by white settlers.

The stories which follow have been taken from different groups who have allowed these stories to be told outside their own group.

· Creation Story ·

We have been told, as our fathers were before us, that there was land, but it was a bare, flat, barren plain. No animals ran there. No birds sang overhead. No trees or bushes grew. No sound of water could be heard. Nor was there any man or woman.

Baiame, or the Maker of Many Things as some call him, brought the Dreamtime ancestors from under the ground and over the seas. With them, life came to the barren, flat plain. Some of the Dreamtime ancestors looked like men or women. Others looked like the animals or creatures which descended from them. But often the Dreamtime ancestors could change their shape. So the Swordfish ancestor could look like a swordfish, or a man or woman.

As the Dreamtime ancestors wandered over the land, many adventures befell them. They met with other ancestors. Arguments often arose and the ancestors would set out on their travels again. They met strange creatures and fought battles. Each time something happened, the very shape of the land changed. Hills arose, plants grew. Where the Barramundi-fish ancestor swam, rivers appeared. When people, ancestors or animals did what they should not, the Rainbow Snake would rush down upon them. He would either drown them, making bays and rivers, or swallow them. Then he would spit out their bones to form rocks and hills. But the Rainbow Snake is not just vengeful. To some peoples the Rainbow Snake is Old Woman, who in the Dreamtime taught her children – humans – to talk and understand, to dig for food, and what to eat.

And the sun, moon and stars? These also came to be in the Dreamtime. For one day Emu ancestor and Eagle ancestor were fighting. Eagle took one of Emu's eggs and threw it into the air. Soaring up, it burst into flames. Baiame fed the flame with wood. So the sun was made, and is made anew each day with fresh wood.

The Dreamtime ancestors taught their groups how to perform secret ceremonies. Then the ancestors sank back into the earth or rose into the sky, but remain ever present.

But Dreamtime is not over. For when ceremonies are performed, Dreamtime comes to those who celebrate, and they learn to see this land as the Dreaming sees it – alive.

· The meaning behind the story ·

The story opens with the land (earth) already in existence. A few stories tell of the land itself being made, but most begin with the land already there. The land is like a stage, upon which the drama of life is performed. Just as no one worries where the stage comes from, so it is with the land.

Many of Australia's Aborigine groups tell of a Maker of Many Things, often called Baiame, who causes the Dreamtime to begin. Dreamtime stories are pictures of how the world came to be, and Baiame means 'to make or build'.

It is the Dreamtime ancestors who bring life and shape to the plain, and who are still there in the hills, rivers, people, birds, insects and animals. One very important thing to notice is that these ancestors are pictured as humans or animals, or sometimes both. This means that members of the groups who have the Long-necked Turtle as their symbol and Dreamtime ancestor see themselves like brothers and sisters to the actual long-necked turtle. They share the same ancestor. So it is only in very rare circumstances that members of this group will kill, or even harm, a long-necked turtle.

The Dreamtime ancestors undergo great journeys and adventures, and as they travel they change the landscape. The ancestors are not exactly superheroes, because often the adventures are the results of accidents or problems.

Before the Dreamtime ancestors return to the earth, they teach their children the secret ceremonies. Through these rituals, new generations learn how and why everything came to be, and will always be. Having

taught this, the Dreamtime ancestors return to where they have come from — rocks, trees, waterholes, the sky. But it would be a big mistake to think that they are dead, or that the Dreamtime is over. The Australian Aborigines believe that the ancestors live, and not just in their descendants. Dreamtime is all around still. It is there for those who know to see — in the hills, deserts, waterholes, rivers, sand, trees, animals, birds, insects and the people themselves. All these tell something of the Dreamtime. And through the secret ceremonies, each new generation is brought into the law which comes from the Dreaming. Then they can understand and become part of the living world.

So what may appear to outsiders as barren, dusty, hilly country is a living, exciting map of life to the Aborigines. What seems to be foreign and alien to outsiders, is to the Aborigine part of himself or herself, as well as he or she being part of it. Through the power of the Dreamtime, the very environment is sacred and alive.

· Way of life ·

The Australian Aborigines see themselves as being linked to the land through the stories and places of the Dreamtime. They do not feel that they own the land, but that the land owns them.

The people are also linked to various creatures by the animal/human Dreamtime ancestors. But perhaps the most important link is made by the Aborigines' special ceremonies. By these, they fulfil their responsibility to the land and all creatures. They are part of it, and without it they would not exist.

For an Aborigine, the land is like a person, as shown by this song:
'Come with me to the point and we'll look at the country,
We'll look across at the rocks,
Look, rain is coming!
It falls on my sweetheart'.

So the land that an Aborigine walks and hunts on is not just rocks and waterholes. It is a sacred land, shaped by the ancestors, and full of power and messages to an Aborigine. Part of that power is inside each person who has discovered Dreaming. The stories are like a map by which the land can be understood, but only by those who know the stories and secrets of the Dreaming. If you understand, then all sorts of things can be found — where water can be dug for, what bushes have roots you can eat, where the best trees for kangaroo spears can be found.

Although the Aborigines live from the land by hunting, fishing and harvesting, there are lots of examples of how they also care for the land and its life. For instance, in the hot, dry desert areas of Australia, the few waterholes which can be found are very precious — precious not just for humans, but also for the wildlife in those areas. It is the job of the humans to clean and clear out the waterholes, to stop them disappearing. And because these special, sacred places are linked to Dreamtime ancestors, they are seen to be safe places for certain animals. So if it is the waterhole where the Goanna ancestor returned to the earth, then you cannot kill or eat goannas there.

Even the seeds from fruit are to be cared for and given a chance of life. It is the custom for the pips and seeds from fruit to be spat out on to special 'compost heaps' at the edge of the camps, where the seeds can grow and provide fruit for people yet to come.

One last point should be made. When a baby is born, the Aborigines see it as being linked to the spirit of a particular Dreamtime ancestor. Which ancestor it is depends on where the baby was born, or to be more precise, where the parents first knew a baby was on the way. In many cases, it is easy to tell, because the parents are at a sacred site of one creature or plant.

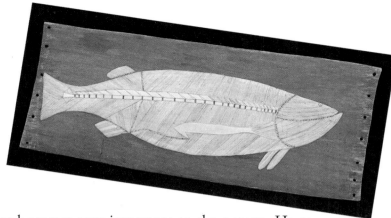

This creature or plant becomes very important to the person. He or she will respect it and not harm it. Often people feel that they have been warned of danger or death, sickness or disaster, by their own creature or plant. So, for the rest of their lives, Aborigines will feel a strong and powerful link not only to their own creature, but also to the sacred place linked with their birth. There are many sad stories of Aborigines suddenly becoming ill and dying when, perhaps hundreds of miles away, their sacred place has been damaged or destroyed by settlers — the white people who can only see an old waterhole, rock or tree-stump.

Much of the traditional Aborigine way of life has been destroyed. The fine balance has been upset. Sacred sites, the places of the Dreamtime ancestors, have been dug up, bulldozed, built over. The idea of belonging to the land has been attacked by ideas of ownership, and the Aborigines have even been hunted by white people. Yet slowly the Aborigines are trying to return to their own very special relationship with the land. Quite simply, they see the land in a completely different way from the white settlers — as life-filled and life-giving.

· Things to think about ·

The Australian Aborigines have their own special way of thinking about and looking at the land they live on. The white settlers also have their own way of looking at the land, which is very different from that of the Aborigines. What do you think are the most important differences between these two ways of seeing the land? Try looking at your own local area in these two different ways.

Although everything began in the Dreamtime, it is not seen as something which happened a long time ago and then finished — it is still going on. In what ways do the Aborigines see the power of the Dreaming still showing itself?

All Aborigine groups have places which are special for them, and animals which they think of as very close to them, like part of their family. Each person in the group has his or her own special animal or plant. How do you think this affects the way Aborigines treat animals and the world around them?

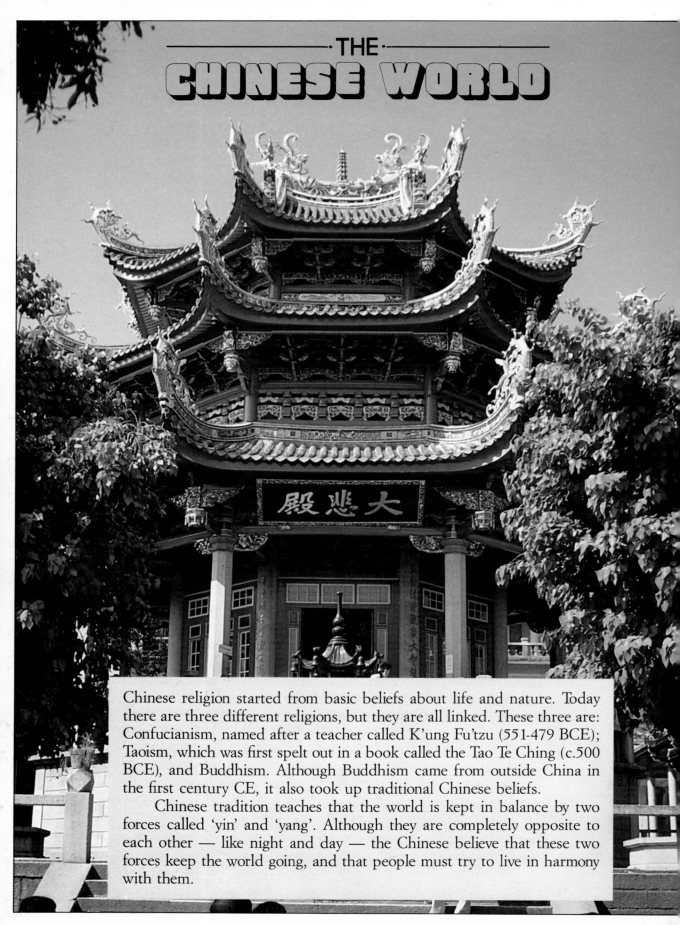

THE CHINESE WORLD

大悲殿

Chinese religion started from basic beliefs about life and nature. Today there are three different religions, but they are all linked. These three are: Confucianism, named after a teacher called K'ung Fu'tzu (551-479 BCE); Taoism, which was first spelt out in a book called the Tao Te Ching (c.500 BCE), and Buddhism. Although Buddhism came from outside China in the first century CE, it also took up traditional Chinese beliefs.

Chinese tradition teaches that the world is kept in balance by two forces called 'yin' and 'yang'. Although they are completely opposite to each other — like night and day — the Chinese believe that these two forces keep the world going, and that people must try to live in harmony with them.

· Creation Story ·

O listener, let it be told of a time when there was nothing but chaos, and that chaos was like a mist and full of emptiness. Suddenly, into the midst of this mist, into this chaos of emptiness, came a great, colourful light. From this light all things that exist came to be. The mist shook and separated. That which was light rose up to form heaven, and that which was heavy sank, and formed the earth.

Now from heaven and earth came forth strong forces. These two forces combined to produce yin and yang. Picture, O listener, this yang like a dragon – hot, fiery, male, full of energy. Imagine, O listener, this yin as a cloud – moist, cool, female, drifting slowly. Each of these forces is full of great power. Left alone, they would destroy the world with their might, and chaos would return. Together, they balance each other, and keep the world in harmony.

This then is yin and yang, and from them came forth everything. The sun is of yang, and the moon, yin. The four seasons and the five elements – water, earth, metal, fire and wood – sprang from them. So did all kinds of living creatures.

So now there was the earth, floating like a jellyfish on water. But the earth was just a ball, without features. Then the forces of yin and yang created the giant figure P'an Ku, the Ancient One. P'an Ku, who never stopped growing every year of his great, long life, set to work to put the earth in order. He dug the river valleys and piled up the mountains. Over many thousands of years he shaped and created the flow and folds of our earth.

But such work took its toll. Even mighty P'an Ku could not escape death, and worn out by his struggle he collapsed and died. His body was now so vast that when he fell to the ground, dead, his body became the five sacred mountains. His flesh became the soil, his bones the rocks, his hair the plants and his blood the rivers. From his sweat came the rain, and from the parasites – the tiny creatures living on his body – came forth human beings.

The people at first lived in caves, but soon Heavenly Emperors came to teach them how to make tools and houses. The people also learned how to build boats, to fish, to plough and plant, and to prepare food. O listener, this is how it all began.

· The meaning behind the story ·

The story opens with chaos, which is felt to be threatening and confusing. Into this murky chaos falls the brilliant light — the opposite of the murky, vague mist. When these two meet, chaos begins to separate, and heaven and earth are created. It is at this point that the two great forces of yin and yang appear.

Life only begins with the two forces of yin and yang. This is the heart of Chinese belief: that everything, from trees and water to animals and people, is composed of yin and yang. They are seen as the male and female forces of the universe. So the sun, hot and forceful, is yang, while the cool, quiet, but powerful moon is yin. But even yin and yang, these great forces that come from the shattering of chaos, are only able to work because the destructive power of each is balanced by the other. Each carries part of the other, and each needs the other to become whole.

To help understand this, the Chinese point to the four seasons. Winter is yin, summer is yang. But winter gives birth to spring — it has to, so summer arises. You cannot have one without the other. They need each other, for without that balance, chaos would reappear.

Looking at the world, the Chinese saw that it was usually people who upset the balance. If, for instance, people mistreat the environment, then the balance is thrown out. The Chinese believe that this can lead to disasters such as great floods, fires, famines, earthquakes or wars. So it can be seen how important it is that yin and yang are balanced.

Now there are many different stories about P'an Ku and who he was. But all the stories make the same point. This child of yin and yang took the earth and brought order to it. The story of P'an Ku goes on to show that for life to really begin on earth, there needs to be something more than just the two powers of yin and yang. There has to be something else. There has to be a act of self-sacrifice. P'an Ku sacrifices himself, gives his life, by working himself to death for the world. It is with the death of P'an Ku that life really begins on earth.

So P'an Ku brings the earth to life. Then the humans who appear learn how to control, use and develop the earth. The Chinese have always

seen the earth as a living being which must be cared for, must be kept in balance, but which also needs to be ordered. People must take care, the story shows, to use the world properly. They must take care to keep the balance, and to keep the world in order.

· Way of life ·

Although the Chinese belief in yin and yang has made people very careful, this does not mean that the Chinese have never tried to experiment or change things. In fact, some of the earliest scientific discoveries took place in China. And, of course, cities have been built, and land farmed. But usually these things have been done with a real sense of responsibility and care for the balance of nature.

One of the earliest forms of Chinese science was concerned with this balance, and the need to build and farm. This skill of working out how to use the land, but also how to keep the harmony, is called 'geomancy' in the West. In Chinese it is '*feng shui*', and means 'wind-water' — examples of yin and yang.

15

In feng shui, even the hills and valleys are seen as living, and having yin and yang within them. To describe their powers, the Chinese picture them as vast, sleeping creatures. Hills and mountains are male, and seen as dragons. So one area in Hong Kong, with nine hills in it, is called Kowloon, meaning 'nine dragons'. The valleys are pictured as female, and seen as tigers. It is the combined strength of these two powerful forces which keeps a place in harmony.

Now, if you see a hill as a sleeping dragon, you will be very careful where and how you build. To stick a large block of flats on the dragon's 'eye' would be to ask for trouble. So you build carefully, making sure you are in harmony with the forces of the hill. And since it is the dragon which offers protection, you do not build higher than the hill — that is to say, above its protection. When it comes to roads, you follow the folds, curves, bends and forces of the land and the rivers.

Just as important is the planting of trees. These are placed to ward off evil forces, and to screen loose rocks which might cause damage. It is often enough just to chop down feng shui trees to bring disaster on your home. So when you come to build, you must examine the land you will work and build upon. You should see it as something which is alive, and not as a dead wasteland. And you must try to leave a site looking as attractive and natural as when you arrived. To do otherwise is to upset nature.

This has not stopped the Chinese developing their land, but they have tried to do it carefully. And it is not just because it makes a more attractive or healthy place to live. It is also important for good fortune. There are many stories of bad luck coming to families who upset the balance of nature.

For the Chinese, the most important time for good feng shui is when they choose a grave site. If the feng shui is bad, then the soul will be unhappy. An unhappy ancestor's soul means bad luck for the family. If the feng shui is good, for example if the site of the grave has a view over water, is on a slope with hills or trees behind and a good wind, then the soul of the dead person will be happy. It will be in harmony with the forces of yin and yang.

Over the hundreds, perhaps thousands of years that feng shui has been practised, the shape of the Chinese landscape has been moulded into gentle lines, with close-packed villages or towns gathered around a hill, or where rivers meet. The planting of trees has meant plenty of wooded hills with a wide range of wildlife. These kind of landscapes have been made famous in Chinese paintings.

Since China became a Communist country in 1949, much has changed. But recently, the ideas in feng shui have been seen as having much to give, even to modern ways of farming and building.

· Things to think about ·

The Chinese say that everything began with chaos — there was no order anywhere. If the forces of yin and yang get out of balance, then chaos will begin to come back. Things may go very wrong in the world, and there may be earthquakes, fires, famines, floods or wars. What do you know about disasters like these? Perhaps you have read about them, or seen them on the television. Sometimes yin and yang may be just a little out of balance — there may be snow and ice, or a summer that is too hot. You may be going on holiday, but the trains may not be running. Write about a time when something like this has happened to you.

The two great forces of yin and yang are opposites — each needs the other to balance it. Yin is seen as cool and quiet, while yang is hot and energetic. Winter and the moon are yin, summer and the sun are yang. Look around you — which of the things you can see would you call yin, and which would you call yang?

The Chinese believe it is important for buildings to fit in well with the land around them, and to be in harmony with the forces in the land. What sort of buildings make you feel comfortable? Are there any sizes or shapes of building that you like best, or any that you feel uncomfortable in?

THE
CHRISTIAN WORLD

Christians are followers of Jesus Christ, who lived in the first century CE. They believe that Jesus was God, and that he became a man to tell people about God's love. Jesus was killed because of his teachings, but Christians believe that he rose from the dead after three days, and is alive today.

After Jesus rose from the dead, Christians believe he returned to heaven. To help his followers, God sent the Holy Spirit. Christians picture God as having three forms or aspects: God the Father, God the Son — who is Jesus, and God the Holy Spirit, who carries out the will of God on earth.

Christians believe that humans have disobeyed God. This disobedience is called sin. But through Jesus, this sin can be forgiven. At the end of time, Christians believe that Jesus will come again, and there will be a New Creation.

· Creation Story ·

Hear how in the beginning, God created heaven and earth. Before this nothing existed but God.

At first the earth was shapeless, darkness covered it, and God's Spirit hovered over the waters. God commanded, *'Let there be light'*, and there was light. God divided the day from the night. This was the first day, and God saw that it was good.

On the second day, God made the heavens to separate the water from the earth, and on the third day he raised the dry land up from the waters below the heavens and commanded the earth to bring forth all plants. God saw that it was good.

God then made the greater light for the day, and the lesser light for the night, and he saw that it was good. This was the fourth day.

On the fifth day, God commanded the waters to fill with living creatures, and the air with birds. He was pleased with what he saw.

On the sixth day, God commanded the earth to bring forth all kinds of living creatures, and he saw that it was good. God then said, *'Let us make man in our own image'*. So God created man and woman in his own likeness, and gave them authority over all living things. God looked at everything he had made, and was pleased.

On the seventh day, God rested.

Now the first man, Adam, was created by God out of soil, and given life by God's breath. Adam named all the animals and the birds, but had no companion of his own. God put him into a deep sleep. Taking one of Adam's ribs, God created woman – Eve. God told them that they could live in the Garden of Eden, eating whatever they wished except the fruit of the tree of knowledge of good and evil.

But the most cunning animal which God had made – the serpent – tempted Eve to eat the forbidden fruit. Adam and Eve ate, and suddenly saw what they had done, and that they were naked. Covering themselves with fig leaves, they tried to hide from God. But God knew of their sin, and called out to them. Then he cursed the serpent, and Adam and Eve, and in shame they were driven from the garden. God told Adam he would now have to labour and sweat to work the very soil from which he had been created. Then God blocked the entrance to the Garden with a fiery sword.

· The meaning behind the story ·

Before anything existed, Christians believe there was God, the Creator and Father of everything. He sent his son, Jesus, to save the world from sin, and his Spirit is ever present. These three are all seen as part of the One God. This is called the Trinity.

Apart from the Trinity, there was nothing. Creation begins when God wishes to create, and from nothing he brings forth everything. The main focus of this story is upon earth and the final creation — human beings. This is captured in the Nicene Creed which is said by most Christians every Sunday in church. A creed is a brief outline of Christian teachings. The Creed starts: *'I believe in one God, the Father Almighty, Maker of heaven and earth and of all things visible and invisible'*.

The story then goes on to the seven days of creation. Some Christians believe that this is exactly what happened — that it took a week. Others see it as a good way of picturing the process of creation, and they do not believe it is an exact description. However, one major point is made in the story — whenever God created, he looked, and saw that it was good. So we know from the story that God was pleased with his creation.

The high point of the story is when God creates human beings. Christians believe humans are very special because they were created in God's image. The story shows that humans were also given power over all living things. Some say that this means people can do whatever they want with the world. But others disagree. They say that this idea is about God giving people a very great responsibility — to care for and look after the world.

With the creation of human beings, God's good creation is now complete and everything is living happily. So what went wrong? Why is there so much suffering and destruction in God's good world? This is the question which the last part of the story tries to answer. It does so by telling the story of the 'fall'. Tempted by the snake, Adam and Eve disobey God,

and the happy state of creation is shattered — nothing is ever the same again. God is pictured driving Adam and Eve from the Garden. God's greatest creation — humans — have sinned, and now all creation suffers as a result. This is the picture that Christians use to help them to understand the world, and why sin, suffering and death have entered it.

It may seem as though God has abandoned the world after this sin. But Christians believe he still cares. They say Jesus was God's son, who came to forgive sin, and to show people how to live as God wants. They believe that this world will end one day, and God will cause a new and better world to arise. In this new world, those who have tried to live as God desires will live for ever.

· Way of life ·

For Christians, God's world is a good place, given for people to live in and have control over. One particular verse in the Bible, in the Old Testament section, captures this Christian idea. In Genesis 1:28, God is pictured as having just finished creation by making man and woman in his own image: *'God blessed them, saying to them, "Be fruitful and multiply, fill the earth and conquer it. Be masters over the fish of the sea, the birds of the air and over all living creatures on the earth".'*

Christian tradition has taught that people are more important than animals, because of this special relationship between God and humanity. The world, with all its living creatures, is there to provide food, drink and shelter for people. But while people are allowed to 'conquer' the natural world, to be masters of all living creatures, this does not mean they should be cruel masters. Certain ways of life have developed from these ideas.

Many people say that the Christian idea of conquering and being masters has led Christians, or countries influenced by Christianity, to see nature as an opponent. The 'conquest of nature' has been a powerful idea. It has led many people and nations to try to discover new ways of taming or using nature to make human life more comfortable.

As industry and the population have increased, so the wild areas of the world have suffered. More and more land has been needed. Trees have been cut down, and animals hunted for their skins and meat. This has been one side of the conquering and mastering of nature. The other side is to be good masters who care for nature. Christians believe that a good master should look after the strong *and* the weak. Most important of all, Christians remember that everything they have, including nature, comes from God.

There are a number of ways in which Christians are reminded of this. We shall look at just two. There are the festivals of thanksgiving for the plants, land, rain and animals which give people their food, shelter and clothing. In Britain this is called Harvest Festival, and is celebrated in the autumn, in late September or early October. People bring all kinds of food and fruit to church on this occasion, to give thanks to God who provides the rain and the sun, the seed and the animals. In America this takes place on Thanksgiving Day, which is the last Thursday in November.

The other important reminder comes in a very special service for Christians. This is Holy Communion or Mass. In this service, bread and wine are shared with everyone, just as Jesus did with his disciples at the Last Supper (Matthew 26:26-29). When the bread and the wine are given to the priest, he reminds the congregation that '*all things come from God*', and that anything given to God, like the bread and the wine, are God's anyway.

Some Christians have tried to encourage others to love and care for the world's wildlife. One such person was St Francis of Assisi, who treated all animals and birds as his brothers and sisters — even preaching to them! Another was St Cuthbert, who turned his island monastery into an animal and bird sanctuary in the seventh century CE.

In the nineteenth century there were two well-known Christian reformers. William Wilberforce brought in Acts of Parliament to stop bull-baiting. He was one of the founders of the Royal Society for the Prevention of Cruelty to Animals. Lord Shaftesbury helped to form what is now called the National Anti-Vivisection Society, which tries to stop experiments on animals.

In this century, the idea of wildlife sanctuaries has grown. The word 'sanctuary' comes from the most holy part of a church, where the altar is kept. In the past, people could hide there to escape punishment. If they were innocent, the church would protect them. So the idea arose of sanctuaries for wildlife, as a protection from people's greed. Some Christians have been involved in setting up such places, believing that this is one way of balancing the conquering of nature with the care of nature.

· Things to think about ·

Christians see the world as a good place, made by a God who loves and cares for the world. They also believe that people are the most important part of creation. How do you think this affects the way that Christians behave?

Although the world that God made is good, people often suffer pain and unhappiness. Christians tell the story of how the first man and woman disobeyed God, to help explain why there are bad things in the world as well as good. Why do you think these things happen?

Some Christians see nature as something which they have to fight, so that they can carry on living as they do. Others see the world and everything in it as something they are here to look after. What do you think?

THE
HINDU WORLD

The Hindu religion is said to have existed in India for many thousands of years. Originally the Persian name for the River Indus, the word 'Hindu' was first used by Muslims to distinguish the religion of the people of India from their own.

One of Hinduism's most important beliefs is in reincarnation. This means that Hindus believe that after death their souls are reborn in another body. The soul may pass through a wide variety of forms of life – animal, bird or human. Each soul is trying to reach the point where it can return to the Supreme One. When the soul reaches this point, it can finally leave the otherwise never-ending cycle of birth, death and rebirth.

These beliefs mean that Hindus have a great respect for all living things.

·Creation Story·

Many stories are told of the cycle of life, but let me explain it to you like this. This is not the first world, nor is it the first universe. There have been, and will be, many more worlds and universes than there are drops of water in the holy river Ganges.

The universes are made by Lord Brahma, the Creator, maintained by Lord Vishnu, the Preserver, and destroyed by Lord Shiva. From the destruction comes new life, so Lord Shiva is the Destroyer and Re-creator. These three gods are all forms of and part of the Supreme One, which is behind and beyond all.

The cycle of creation, life, destruction and new creation happens thus. After the old universe is destroyed, nothing is left but a vast ocean. Floating on this, on the great snake Ananta, is Lord Vishnu. Some say that a lotus flower springs from his navel, and from this comes Lord Brahma.

How does Lord Brahma create? Some tell of how he grows lonely, and splits himself in two to create male and female. Then he becomes one again, and human beings are created. In the same way, he creates all the other living creatures, from the great animals to the tiniest insects. Others say that everything comes from different parts of Lord Brahma's body. Everything comes from one – Lord Brahma, who is part of the Supreme One – so everything comes from the Supreme One. At the end of this universe, all will return to the Supreme One. For this universe, this world, and this Lord Brahma, like all those before and all those to come, will be destroyed by Lord Shiva.

How long is the life of a universe? Its length is beyond imagination. One day to Lord Brahma is longer than four thousand million of our years. Every night when Lord Brahma sleeps, the world is destroyed. Every morning when he awakes, it is created again.

When the Lord Brahma of this universe has lived a lifetime of such days, the universe is completely destroyed by Lord Shiva. For an unimaginable period of time, chaos and water alone exist. Then once again, Lord Vishnu appears, floating on the vast ocean. From Lord Vishnu comes forth Lord Brahma of the new universe, and the cycle continues – for ever.

· The meaning behind the story ·

What a tremendous picture of time these stories give! Not only is this world seen as just one of the countless many – even the universe is seen as just one in an endless line of universes. These are created and then destroyed, only to be replaced by new universes. The Ganges, India's holiest and greatest river, is mentioned in the story to try to show the vast number of worlds and universes there have been, and how many more there will be. Hindus believe that just as the water in the River Ganges flows without stopping, so life itself continues with each new world and each new universe.

It is very hard for us to imagine things happening on this scale. Perhaps that is one of the most important ideas behind this story – that the Supreme One is beyond human understanding.

These stories speak of how the world and the universe were made, and how they will also be destroyed – just a part of the cycle or wheel of life.

There are three important figures in the stories. Hindus believe that the three are all part of the Supreme One, and show different actions of the Supreme One. They are Lord Brahma, the Creator; Lord Vishnu, the Preserver, and Lord Shiva, the Destroyer and Re-creator.

Lord Brahma is seen as the Creator, because he begins the cycle of the universe by creating everything. There are many different stories explaining how he does this, some of which are given in the story, but all of them show that everything comes from the one source.

When Lord Brahma has created the universe, Lord Vishnu preserves it. He makes sure that the process of creation is kept going.

Lord Shiva completes the cycle. Hindus believe that he destroys the universe because its time has come. But Lord Shiva is not just the Destroyer. From this destruction, the whole cycle starts again, and new creation is possible. Lord Shiva is sometimes shown as the Lord of the Dance, keeping the cycle of life going by destruction, creation, destruction, and so on.

The idea of everything being part of a cycle is very important to Hindus. There is the vast cycle of the universe, the smaller cycle of the world, and the tiny cycles of all living things. Each living thing is believed to have a soul, called the 'atman', which is reborn time and time again. Even the universe and the Creator, Lord Brahma, are reborn. And everything is filled with the same power – the Supreme One.

Because everything is part of the Supreme One, Hindus believe that every living thing is equally important in the great cycle of life.

· Way of life ·

For the Hindu, everything – animal, bird or human – is part of the Supreme One. Hindus also believe in reincarnation – that after death, the soul is reborn in a new body. What kind of body the soul is reborn into depends on how your life has been lived. The more wicked and selfish you have been, the more likely you are to be reborn as an animal or insect. But if you try to live a good life, you can eventually escape being reborn in this world, and return to the Supreme One.

This belief that the soul can be reborn into another form means that Hindus see all life as sacred — it is all part of the Supreme One. So, many Hindus believe that it is wrong to eat meat, because that means killing animals. Instead, Hindus eat a wide range of fruits, pulses, grains and vegetables. Since vegetables are such an important part of their diet, Hindus are called vegetarians. The idea behind vegetarianism is respect for all life. Many Hindus believe that if there are other ways of getting food – such as gathering wild fruits, growing vegetables, keeping cows – then there is no need to kill animals.

In India, Hindus will never hurt or kill a cow. It is seen as a very special animal, and often called 'the mother' because it can produce so much for the family. The cow's milk can be made into yoghurt and curds, and it can also provide oil for cooking and for lamps. The cow's dung can be used as fuel, and its urine for building purposes. And it is the strength of the bull which pulls the plough, to help the family grow their crops. So to kill a cow just for its meat would be stupid. A dead cow cannot give as much as a living cow!

This has led to the cow being seen as a very important symbol of the care which must exist between humans and all other animals. In India, cows roam freely through the streets, and no Hindu will harm one. The great Indian leader, Mahatma Gandhi, said, '*In its finer or spiritual sense, the term "cow-protection" means the protection of every living creature*'.

This duty to care for all living things is part of 'dharma'. Dharma is a very hard word to explain, but we can translate it as 'duty'. If we as human beings do our duty, then we create what is called good 'karma'. Karma is the result, the product, of what we do. Let's look at an example to see what dharma and karma mean.

A big hamburger firm recently advertised that they had served many billions of hamburgers. Now to Hindus that is a boast. It means that millions of animals have been killed just to feed people. Just think of all

that suffering! And it also means that in South America, the rain forests are slowly being destroyed to make bigger areas of grazing land for cattle, before they are slaughtered. In turn, this changes the very delicate balance of the earth's environment. Less rain, more poisonous fumes, not to mention all the wildlife that suffers or is lost too. So in the end, we are only hurting ourselves. Our lack of dharma, of duty towards other creatures, is bad karma – bad action.

For Hindus, this is very important. If someone dies with bad karma, then their souls will not be reborn in a human body. That person is more likely to be reborn as a lower creature, without the responsibilities that humans have.

So Hindus see humans as linked to all life. All life comes from the Supreme One, and is reborn time and time again, until the soul returns to the Supreme One. In the Isa Upanishad, an ancient and important book of Hinduism, it says: '*Everything in the Universe, living creatures or rocks or waters, belongs to the Lord. You shall therefore only take what is really necessary for yourself, your quota. You should not take anything else, because you know to whom it really belongs*'.

· Things to think about ·

As you can see from the story, Hindus believe that the idea of life happening in cycles or circles is very important. When you look at your own life, can you think of any cycles which happen around you, for example in your family, your school or the place where you live?

Everything in the cycle comes from the Supreme One, and goes back to the Supreme One. Everything, in fact, is part of the Supreme One, and so Hindus believe that all living things are equal. What effects do you think this has on Hindus and the way they treat the world around them?

Think about Hindu ideas and beliefs. If people believe all living things are equal, how might this change the way they eat? Try to plan a meal which would show respect for all living things.

· THE ·
HUMANIST WORLD

Humanist ideas began many thousands of years ago in the civilization of ancient Greece. In the last two hundred years, as scientific knowledge has grown, Humanist ideas have developed.

Humanists believe that everything which exists is a result of natural processes, and that in time modern science will be able to explain how all these processes work. Humanists believe that because humans are the most intelligent creatures, they are responsible for caring for the world. As humans grow in knowledge and understanding, they become more and more responsible for the development of life on earth.

Humanists get their name from their belief in and concern for humanity. The creation story which follows is the one given by modern science, and which Humanists believe is on the right lines.

· Creation Story ·

The beginning of the world may be hard to understand, but science can explain much of it, and is always trying to understand more.

'In the beginning . . .' – or was there a beginning? Some people think that the universe didn't begin, because it is full of energy which never stops. This energy goes through cycles, which means that the universe is continually expanding, collapsing and expanding again. Others think that the universe began with a 'big bang'. But all these people agree that the universe is always changing.

Over twelve billion years ago, the universe was a mass of vast, hot, swirling clouds of gas. Planets, stars, suns and galaxies were formed as the gases cooled. Countless millions of stars were made.

Our own galaxy, the Milky Way, was made like this. It has millions of stars. Our sun is one, out towards the edge of the galaxy. Many gases swirled around the sun as it began to form. From these gases, the earth and all the other planets in the solar system were made. This happened over four and a half thousand million years ago.

Then ultra-violet light from the sun, along with electricity from thunderstorms and great heat from the violently erupting volcanoes on earth, caused the gases and waters to produce the earliest forms of life. For millions of years, these single cells slowly developed. They formed many-celled things, then more complicated living things. So began the journey of life which is called evolution.

New living things appeared because of changes which the earth went through, because of changes in the cells themselves. Those which fitted in best with their surroundings were the most likely to live and give birth to the next generation.

Life spread from the waters on to the land and into the air. Some creatures, like the dinosaurs, have died out. Some appear to have remained unchanged for millions of years. Others have evolved to give the present amazing range of living creatures.

So, over the years, different forms of life have evolved. We humans, along with the apes, have evolved from a common ancestor. But now humans have powers which can either improve or destroy the world. This means that the future of the earth depends on what we choose to do.

· The meaning behind the story ·

This story of how the world and living things were made looks at the natural forces of the universe. Humanists believe that these forces, like the wind or the rain, work in certain ways because that is in their nature. So this story tries to explore how and why things have happened.

Was there a time before the universe existed? Those who believe in the 'big bang' idea say that there was a time before the universe began – the time before the 'big bang'. Others say that the universe has always existed because of the force called energy. Since energy never disappears, the universe has always been there.

Although there are two ideas about where everything comes from, Humanists agree that the universe is always changing. As the story tells us, it is continually expanding, collapsing and expanding again. The distances between galaxies, let alone the size of the universe, are so unimaginably huge as to make our heads spin.

Let's turn to our own galaxy, called the Milky Way. Humanists believe that the stars, suns and planets were slowly formed out of the swirling clouds of gases. Towards the edge of the Milky Way lies our sun, with the earth revolving around it.

So far the story has told of how the galaxy and its stars, suns and planets were made. It is only after the birth of the earth that living things begin to appear. But how are these living things made? The story explains that a mixture of different ingredients caused tiny, living cells to be formed. After a very long time, these tiny cells became collections of cells. Eventually, very early simple living things were formed.

As these simple life forms reproduce, sometimes small but important changes take place. Most of these changes, which are called 'mutations', weaken the creatures, which then die. But some changes are good, and help to make the creatures more suited to their surroundings. As the creatures become stronger, they begin to take over the others. It is thought that changes like this happen fairly regularly over vast periods of time, as life forms evolve and become more and more complicated and different.

It is believed that human beings are one of the results of this process of evolution, and are among the most recent of all the creatures which have evolved. Since human beings are also the most intelligent animal Humanists think that they should use this knowledge to think and care for other animals, and the earth itself.

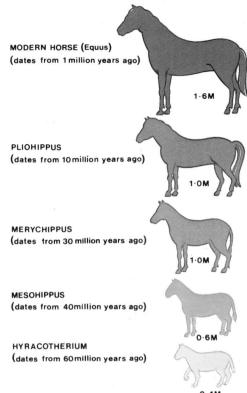

MODERN HORSE (Equus)
(dates from 1 million years ago)
1·6M

PLIOHIPPUS
(dates from 10 million years ago)
1·0M

MERYCHIPPUS
(dates from 30 million years ago)
1·0M

MESOHIPPUS
(dates from 40 million years ago)
0·6M

HYRACOTHERIUM
(dates from 60 million years ago)
0·4M

EVOLUTION OF A HORSE

· Way of life ·

The scientific story, which Humanists accept, is about the growth of life from single cells to more complicated forms of life. This is called evolution. The Humanist believes that because humans are the only animals that can really be responsible for what they do, they are the most advanced form of life.

A hungry lion does not think about whether it ought to kill a zebra – only his instinct for survival makes him do it. People can decide to kill a zebra whether they are hungry or not.

The creation story shows how Humanists believe that all living things are the result of millions of years of evolution. Everything is linked together to form a balanced world. This should teach us respect and care, not just for humans, but for all living things.

But can humans really care for this world? If we look around, we can see terrible cruelty, destruction and greed. This is destroying our planet, poisoning our plants, killing the animals, and humans too. But Humanists see all this, and do not give up hope.

Just as humans have evolved from simpler creatures, so the ways that humans organize themselves have changed over hundreds of thousands of years. In early times, humans organized themselves as tribes, living in small groups, hunting and fishing. Life was tough. But because humans were still weak and very few, they were not a real threat to nature.

Over thousands of years, the tribes grew into states, kingdoms or empires. These in turn became nations. The organizations grew bigger, and the number of human beings grew. The risks of the destruction of nature, as well as the chances for people to use resources for the good of everyone, also became greater. Humanists know that all animals have always used the environment. There is nothing wrong in that. What Humanists do say is that now we are so powerful, we must think and plan carefully how to use the environment. This is something that a beaver, tiger or chimpanzee never has to do.

Humanists are strong supporters of organizations which bring together human beings from all nations – to work together, to be responsible together. Many Humanists have seen the next step in human evolution as being One Government for the whole world. For instance, through the United Nations, Humanists believe that we can plan a good future for all life on earth, as well as stop the greed which threatens to destroy it. The same knowledge which can help us to feed or clothe all the people in the world, can also kill us all.

Many famous Humanists have given much of their time and energy to this work. An example of this is Sir Julian Huxley. As a zoologist, he was very concerned with animals. He helped to set up Whipsnade Zoo so that we could study animals, breed endangered species and learn from them. Because he believed in evolution, he felt that we humans might understand ourselves better if we could see from where we had evolved. He also helped to found the World Wildlife Fund to save animals which were being wiped out in their own countries.

Huxley also helped to set up a very important organization – the United Nations Educational, Scientific and Cultural Organization. This organization tries to bring together people whose knowledge can help the world in all sorts of ways – food, water, peace, education, conservation. UNESCO was not just started by Humanists, and Humanists are not the only ones who work for it. People from all kinds of religious, cultural and political backgrounds work together. This is the way that Humanists believe we must evolve if the great problems which face not only human beings, but all life, are to be solved.

Humanists try to help people to see what needs to be done to help the world. Through many organizations, through exploring nature and science, they hope people will come to understand more about life and evolution. Only then will people understand what a big responsibility we have – the responsibility for life on earth.

· Things to think about ·

Humanists talk about how the universe was created by natural processes. These processes are going on all the time. Think about the things which happen around you. Which of these do you think are good examples of natural processes?

Humanists believe that although living things have changed or evolved from simple forms, most of them are not as advanced as human beings. This is because they are not able to make reasoned choices about what they do. A lion does not decide to kill a zebra; he kills because he is hungry. Can you think of other examples of the way that animals act which shows that they are not really responsible for their actions?

Humanists believe that humans can make choices and are responsible for what they do, so they must use their intelligence to do things which help the world, instead of harming it. What difference does this make to the way that we live? What difference do you think it *should* make?

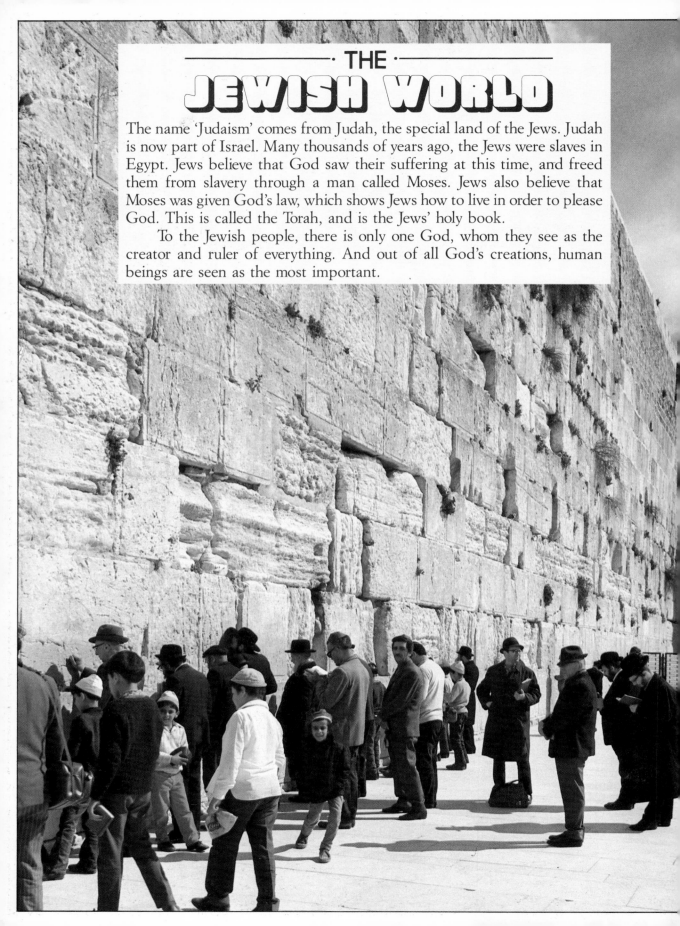

· THE ·
JEWISH WORLD

The name 'Judaism' comes from Judah, the special land of the Jews. Judah is now part of Israel. Many thousands of years ago, the Jews were slaves in Egypt. Jews believe that God saw their suffering at this time, and freed them from slavery through a man called Moses. Jews also believe that Moses was given God's law, which shows Jews how to live in order to please God. This is called the Torah, and is the Jews' holy book.

To the Jewish people, there is only one God, whom they see as the creator and ruler of everything. And out of all God's creations, human beings are seen as the most important.

· Creation Story ·

Come listen to the tale the Torah tells, of how in the beginning God created the heavens and the earth. Some say that God also created the Torah at this time, and a mighty voice crying, *'Return'*.

God said, *'Let there be light'*, and there was light. God saw that it was good. God divided the light from the darkness, naming them 'day' and 'night'. Evening and morning came – the first day.

God said, *'Let the waters be divided'*. God made the arch of the sky to hold back the waters from the earth. He placed some above the arch, and some below. Legend says the waters argued about this, and disagreement entered the universe. Of this day God did not say, *'It is good'*. Evening and morning came – the second day.

God said, *'Let the waters under heaven come together, and dry land appear'*. The earth arose, and plants and trees grew, and God saw that it was good. Evening and morning came – the third day.

God said, *'Let the great light and the small light appear in heaven to govern day and night'*. God saw that it was good. Evening came and morning came – the fourth day.

God said, *'Let the waters fill with creatures and the sky with birds'*. God saw that it was good, and blessed them. Evening came and morning came – the fifth day.

God said, *'Let the earth bring forth every kind of living creature'*. God saw that it was good. Then, last of all, when the earth was ready, God said, *'Let us take dust and create man, Adam, to be master over all creatures'*. So Adam was created in God's own image.

God saw that Adam needed a friend – woman. Some say that the earth was worried, and asked, *'How shall I feed all her children?'* God replied, *'Fear not, together we shall find food'*. So Lilith was made from the dust, also in God's image. Lilith would not live with Adam, and went her own way. So God made a woman before Adam's eyes, but Adam turned away. God put Adam in a deep sleep and made Eve from one of Adam's ribs. He placed the couple in Paradise.

On the seventh day, God finished his work and rested.

And Paradise was blissful, until Adam and Eve ate fruit from the tree of knowledge of good and evil, which God had forbidden. God punished them, casting them out to struggle in this earthly life.

· The meaning behind the story ·

The Torah story from Genesis 1 and 2 is really very basic, but Jewish stories and traditions have grown up around it. There are many of them: some are given in the story, and some here. The stories are traditional ways of explaining and trying to understand the creation. Indeed, some rabbis have said that no one should study this text alone, for fear of the great questions that it raises.

The story starts with '*In the beginning, God ...*'. For the Jewish people, all life and all creation has a definite start. The cause of everything is God, and God is portrayed as creating the world in seven days.

Many people argue about the meaning of the word 'day' in this story. Is it just twenty-four hours, or is it a poetic way of describing a longer period? Whatever the answer, the story is really about the progress of creation. The idea of days in a week is a useful way of imagining the progress. For Jews, each day begins and ends with the setting of the sun, perhaps because the story says '*Evening came and morning came*' on each of the days of creation. By looking at what happens each 'day', we can see the steady growth of creation – from light and dark to animals and humans.

Jews see human beings as God's most important creation, and one particular Jewish tradition helps to explain why. This tradition says that when Adam was created, the angels were very upset and asked why Adam was needed. God replied, '*The birds of the air and fishes of the sea, what are they created for? What use is a larder full of delicious foods if there is no guest to enjoy them?*'

Another tradition tells of the earth complaining when God decides to make woman. The earth is worried about feeding all her children. But God assures the earth that it will be possible. Perhaps the earth is still worried, as the human population continues to grow.

Finally there is Paradise. Jews believe that Paradise was the perfect creation, with man and woman living in wonderful happiness with all the other creatures. God sets one condition – that Adam and Eve do not eat from the tree of knowledge of good and evil. But they do, and Paradise is shattered. From Paradise, Adam and Eve are sent out into the world. Then suffering, killing, disease and sadness fall upon the earth. But Jews think that God has prepared for this. The voice calling 'Return'; the Torah showing the way for people to live to please God, and something called repentance, which means returning to obeying God's will – all of these are there to help people to come back to God. And Jews believe that the perfect creation will come again when God sends his Messiah – the promised saviour.

· Way of life ·

As we saw in the creation story, trees play quite an important part. There are the trees on the third day. There are the trees in Paradise which provide their fruit for Adam and Eve. There is the tree of knowledge of good and evil. Jews believe that the world has been created for the pleasure of people and God. All the goodness of it is there to be enjoyed. And, of course, one of the greatest sources of food and materials is trees.

In the hot, desert areas which surround and are part of Israel, the lack of trees is a sign of death. So it is hardly surprising that Judaism has

always taught the proper care, use and respect of trees. For instance, in the Torah we find very strict instructions on how to treat an enemy's trees during war. In Deuteronomy 20:19, it says: *'When you besiege a city ... you shall not destroy its trees ... for you may eat of them but not cut them down. Are the trees in the field men, that they should be besieged by you?'*

There are many festivals in Judaism which remind Jews of how God, through the riches of nature, feeds and cares for humans and all living things. The three great festivals of Passover, Shavuot and Succot are all harvest celebrations, giving thanks to God for different crops. Even in the midst of cities, at Succot Jews will build temporary huts from branches, and fill them with fruits and grains. This reminds them of the time in the desert, called the Exodus. It also recalls how everyone needs the fruit and trees to live.

There is one festival which is particularly important for the environment. On the fifteenth day of the Hebrew month Shevat (mid to late January in the Western calendar), comes the New Year festival for trees. Called Tu B'Shevat (which means the fifteenth day of Shevat), or Rosh Hashanah L'ilanot (New Year for trees), it is celebrated by Jews worldwide as a day for planting trees. Nowadays many families, schools and communities will not just plant trees in their own area, be that downtown New York or rural Australia. They will also collect money to be given for trees to be planted in Israel.

These tree-planting days of Tu B'Shevat have not only made the cities where Jews live more beautiful, but have helped to reclaim parts of the land which were desert in Israel. This has been going on for many years, before the modern state of Israel came to be, although since 1948 it has increased greatly.

Through this tree-planting programme, the spirit of Tu B'Shevat is captured. Jews believe God has created a good world, and that we must

care for it. There is a story in the Midrash which shows why. The Midrash is a collection of stories and commentaries in the Talmud.

'Adam walked in the Garden on the first day. He smelled wonderful scents and enjoyed the beautiful sight. The aroma of the ripened fruit drew him to the trees. He reached for an apricot that hung from a branch. The fruit lifted itself so that he could not touch it. He reached for a pomegranate. The fruit evaded his hand. Then a voice spoke, "Till the soil and care for the trees and then you may eat".'

When Moses, the founder leader of Israel, first heard God speak (Exodus 3), God promised him that he would care for the people of Israel for ever. But the people of Israel must be loving and faithful in return. This concern for those who are living, as well as those still to come, is also captured in the Jewish care for trees. Here is another story from the Midrash:

'A wise rabbi was walking along a road when he saw a man planting a tree. The rabbi asked him, "How many years will it take for this tree to bear fruit?" The man answered that it would take seventy years. The rabbi asked, "Are you so fit and strong that you expect to live that long and eat its fruit?" The man answered, "I found a fruitful world because my forefathers planted for me. So I will do the same for my children".'

· Things to think about ·

Jews believe that the world is here for a reason. It was created because God had a reason for wanting it to be here. How do you think this affects the way that Jews see the world around them?

One Jewish story says that the world is like a larder for people to use. Think about this idea of a larder — larders are not much use if they are not kept filled. Do you think comparing the world with a larder helps you to think about how to treat the world?

Trees are very important to Jews. Look around where you live, and see if there are any trees there. Do you think that people who live in your area think trees are important or not? What reasons do people give in your area for having trees — decoration, food, climbing, shade, cleaning the air, or what?

THE
MUSLIM WORLD

The word 'Islam' means submission or peace. Those who practise this religion are called Muslims. Muslims believe that there is only one God, and that people should follow, or submit, to God's will. God's will has been revealed at different times to different prophets. Muslims believe that the prophet Muhammad (born 570 CE) was the last prophet, and that the message given to him by God was the last one. This message is written down in the Qur'an, the holy book of Islam.

The Qur'an teaches that God created everything. Although God made humans superior to the rest of creation, the Qur'an also teaches that Muslims should be thankful for all living things, since God is the creator of all life.

· Creation Story ·

How did everything come to be? I will tell you as I have heard it.

In the time before time, God was. And when God wants to create something, all he needs to say is 'Be', and it becomes. So it was that God created the world and the heavens. He made all the creatures which walk, swim, crawl and fly on the face of the earth. He made the angels, and the sun, moon and stars to dwell in the universe.

And consider, as the Qur'an says, how God poured down the rain in torrents, and broke up the soil to bring forth the corn, the grapes and other vegetation; the olive and the palm, the fruit trees and the grass.

Then it was that God ordered the angels to go to the earth, and to bring seven handfuls of soil, all of different colours, from which he could model man. God took the seven kinds of earth, and moulded them into a model of a man. He breathed life and power into it, and it immediately sprang to life. And this first man was called Adam.

God took Adam to live in Paradise. In Paradise, God created Eve, the first woman, from out of Adam's side. God taught Adam the names of all the creatures, and then commanded the angels to bow down before Adam. But Iblis, one amongst the angels, refused to do this, and thus began to disobey God's will.

God placed the couple in a beautiful garden in Paradise, telling them that they could eat whatever they wanted, except the fruit of one forbidden tree. But the evil one tempted them to disobey God, and eat the fruit. When God knew that Adam and Eve had disobeyed him, he cast them out of Paradise, and sent them to earth.

But God is merciful. The earth was created to give food, drink and shelter to the human race. The sun, moon and stars give light. It is a good world, where everything has been created to serve people. And people, the Qur'an teaches, should serve God and obey his will. For those who submit to the will of God will be saved, and taken to live for ever in Paradise.

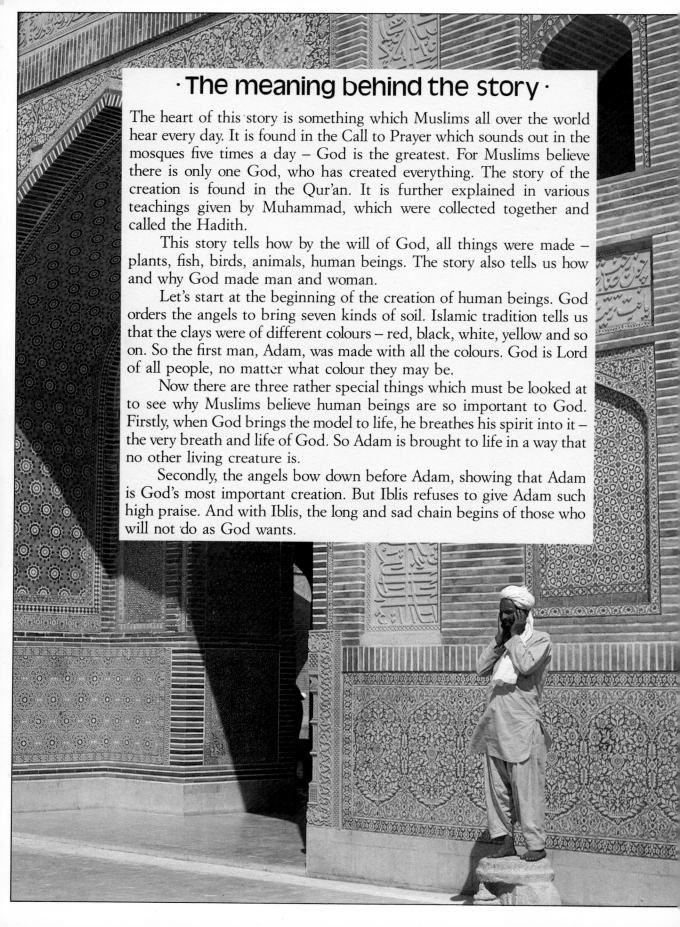

· The meaning behind the story ·

The heart of this story is something which Muslims all over the world hear every day. It is found in the Call to Prayer which sounds out in the mosques five times a day – God is the greatest. For Muslims believe there is only one God, who has created everything. The story of the creation is found in the Qur'an. It is further explained in various teachings given by Muhammad, which were collected together and called the Hadith.

This story tells how by the will of God, all things were made – plants, fish, birds, animals, human beings. The story also tells us how and why God made man and woman.

Let's start at the beginning of the creation of human beings. God orders the angels to bring seven kinds of soil. Islamic tradition tells us that the clays were of different colours – red, black, white, yellow and so on. So the first man, Adam, was made with all the colours. God is Lord of all people, no matter what colour they may be.

Now there are three rather special things which must be looked at to see why Muslims believe human beings are so important to God. Firstly, when God brings the model to life, he breathes his spirit into it – the very breath and life of God. So Adam is brought to life in a way that no other living creature is.

Secondly, the angels bow down before Adam, showing that Adam is God's most important creation. But Iblis refuses to give Adam such high praise. And with Iblis, the long and sad chain begins of those who will not do as God wants.

Thirdly, Adam and Eve's first home was not on earth. When they were living as God wished them to, they lived in Paradise. But when they disobeyed God, he took them from Paradise and sent them to live on earth.

You might think that this means the earth is a place of punishment. But the Qur'an teaches that it is a lovely place, specially built by God to give humans food, warmth, drink and beauty. If things go wrong with people's lives, it is not God's fault, nor the fault of the earth. It is because people still disobey God's will. When people suffer, the world and all its creatures suffer too, for Muslims believe that God has given humans power over all living things. The world is here to be enjoyed, but also to be cared for as part of God's creation. To a Muslim, to treat animals badly, or to pollute the earth, is another way of disobeying God's will.

· Way of life ·

Muslims believe that God's world is a good world. When people obey God, when they submit to God, life is good. The word 'Islam' means submission. Muslims believe that people are God's greatest creation, and that we have been given everything on earth to care for and look after. The world is not ours to do with as we want. It does not belong to us, but to God. What we use of this world has been given to us on trust. We must answer for all we do to God.

The Qur'an teaches that animals have their own feelings which God cares about: *'There is not an animal that lives on earth, nor a being that flies on wings, which isn't living in communities like you. We have left out nothing in Our Book and they will all be gathered before their Lord in the end'* (Surah 6).

God cares so much for all his creation that *'not a leaf falls without his knowledge'*. Because God cares so much, it is the solemn duty of people to use only what is really needed, and never to waste anything. There is a saying in the Hadith, the stories and teachings of Muhammad, that even if you are sitting on a river, never use more water than you actually need. Even at harvest time, you must never waste food by taking too much, *'for God loveth not the wasters'*.

From this comes the Muslim view of hunting. Muslims enjoy food as a gift from God. But no Muslim should hunt just for pleasure. Hunting is only allowed for food which is really needed. To Muslims, fox or other hunting is very wrong. These animals are only being hunted for the fun of human beings.

The same is true of such sports as cock-fighting, and many Muslims feel that shutting animals up in cages, or putting them in a circus, is very wrong. It is making animals, who, as the Qur'an teaches, have their own families and communities, behave in unnatural ways.

There is a story in the Hadith which illustrates this. One day Muhammad was travelling with some friends. When they stopped for a rest, Muhammad went off by himself for a while. His friends saw a mother bird and her young ones flying in the sky. The friends decided

to catch the young birds to amuse themselves. It didn't take long because the young birds were not very good at flying. Soon the birds were caught, and the men enjoyed feeling the birds struggling against their hands. But when Muhammad returned, he was angry. He could see that the mother bird was upset. He ordered his friends to let the young birds go. Their selfish pleasure had caused great unhappiness to the birds, and that was wrong.

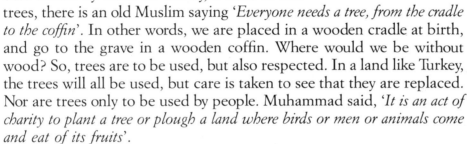

For Muslims, the world and all its wonders are here to serve humanity, the greatest of God's creations. But greatness is best shown by care. In Turkey, a land of few trees, there is an old Muslim saying '*Everyone needs a tree, from the cradle to the coffin*'. In other words, we are placed in a wooden cradle at birth, and go to the grave in a wooden coffin. Where would we be without wood? So, trees are to be used, but also respected. In a land like Turkey, the trees will all be used, but care is taken to see that they are replaced. Nor are trees only to be used by people. Muhammad said, '*It is an act of charity to plant a tree or plough a land where birds or men or animals come and eat of its fruits*'.

The world God created is to be used. But it is how it should be used that Islam tries to teach. If people waste it, spoil it, take from it without replacing; if people use animals or birds for amusement or destroy the communities of living creatures, then they are acting in a way that offends God. Muslims believe we are here to care for God's world as his representatives. We do not have the right to misuse or abuse it.

· Things to think about ·

The word 'Islam' means 'submission'; it also means 'peace'. Muslims believe that God is all-powerful, and they also believe that he is as caring and loving as he is powerful. Why do you think they call their belief a name which means 'submission' and 'peace'?

Muslims believe that people who do cruel and heartless things are disobeying the will of God. What do you think Muslims believe God wants people to do on earth?

Muslims believe that animals have their own feelings and ways of life. Think about this, and then say why a Muslim might think that keeping animals in a circus was not a good thing to do.

· THE YANOMAMO ·
SANEMA WORLD

The Sanema people are one of a number of tribes living in the Amazonian rain forests of South America. They are part of the Yanomamo group of tribes. Each tribe has its own collection of stories. These have been handed down by story-telling from generation to generation.

The Sanema believe that all the living things of the forest came into being because of original ancestors. The spirits of these ancestors are believed to still inhabit the forest.

In recent years, the Sanema's age-old hunter-gatherer way of life has been greatly threatened by outside people moving into the forest, destroying the trees and animals.

· Creation Story ·

Come, sit close, and hear how there once lived Curare-woman and Original Jaguar. Now Jaguar was very fond of meat, and one day he caught Waipili the frog. Jaguar made Curare-woman cut up Waipili and Jaguar ate the frog up. But Curare-woman saved two tadpoles, called Omao and Soawe. She hid them in a pot.

Curare-woman kept Omao and Soawe safe from Jaguar. They grew fast, but Original Jaguar was still a threat. One day, Omao fooled Jaguar into climbing a tree. When released from the hold of a vine, the tree threw Jaguar into the air and he was killed.

Now Omao was hungry because he did not know how to grow yuca. Only Lalagi-gi, the cosmic anaconda, knew how to grow plants. Although Omao was very frightened of Lalagi-gi, he wanted to learn how to grow yuca. So he gave some meat to the snake. In return, Lalagi-gi brought yuca cuttings, yams, maize and other things. Without Lalagi-gi, people would not know how to grow crops.

It was long, long ago that Omao created the Sanema ancestors. He decided to use hardwood trees. But Omao had great difficulty finding them, so he asked his brother Soawe to help. Soawe was lazy. Instead of hardwood trees, he cut down softwood trees.

When Omao returned, he was very angry. *'I was going to make humans from the hardwood trees'*, he said. *'Then they could live for ever, just casting off their old skins. I was going to make the anacondas from the softwood trees, so that they would be weak and die young'*. Omao was so angry that he made the people, the Sanema, from the softwood trees, which is why people are weak and do not live for ever. Then he made the anacondas from the tough bark of the hardwood trees, which is why anacondas shed their skins and live for a long time. Omao was still angry, so he left the world. Way, way down river he went to the bottom of the sky.

It was night when the animal and Sanema ancestors appeared. Sunrise did not come. The great curassow bird cried out all night – and dawn did not come. The ancestors realized that it was the curassow bird which stopped the dawn, so they shot the bird with arrows. The feathers of the dying bird fell off, and changed into all the birds that now live in the forest. And the dawn came.

· The meaning behind the story ·

The Sanema people live in the forests of South America, around some of the large rivers which flow into the Amazon. It is a world full of great trees, brilliantly-coloured noisy birds, and wild animals such as the jaguar; a world of rivers where the mighty anaconda snake lives, and of loud, croaking frogs. So it is not surprising that all these appear in Sanema stories as things which have always been there.

The story opens with Curare-woman and Original Jaguar. This is an important point. The Sanema believe that in the early days of the world, all the creatures and birds had ancestors – originals – who were human-like. It was only because of certain events, accidents or changes that these 'human' ancestors became the originals of the animals, birds, plants and insects which now fill the jungle. For instance, Curare-woman eventually becomes the curare vine.

The Sanema believe that while the human-type ancestors became the creatures and plants of the forest, the Sanema, the true human beings, were created in a very different way. Along with the mighty anaconda snake, they were made by Omao. They were made from the very trees which still surround the Sanema in the forest. This is important because the Sanema see themselves as different from the rest of the forest life and the story tries to show this difference.

The Sanema believe that the spirits of these animal and plant ancestors are still in the forest. These ancestor spirits are called 'hekula', and are very important. They are a force in nature which special people amongst the Sanema can call upon. The people believe that when they kill or gather food, they release the ghosts of the animals and plants. These

ghosts, especially of animals which have been killed, seek revenge. Illness is often seen as being the work of one of these vengeful spirits. Through the special people in the tribe, called 'shamans' by outsiders, the powers of the hekula are called upon to help fight off these ghost illnesses.

This idea that the world of nature is a living and powerful force, created by ancestors and inhabited by spirits, runs throughout Sanema stories. Dependence upon and respect for the forest lie at the heart of these stories. This is captured in the story of cosmic anaconda Lalagi-gi. Very much to be feared, even by Omao, it is Lalagi-gi who teaches Omao and his people how to live from the fruits of the forest. And the forest is a world which must be handled with respect, care and caution.

· Way of life ·

All around the Sanema people lies the vast jungle with its great rivers and wild animals. For the Sanema, this is what life and the landscape is like. They could not really imagine a world without trees, water and all kinds of creatures. It is a dangerous world. Jaguars and snakes, flooding rivers and sudden landslides are a constant threat to life and safety. But it is also a world where everything that is needed for daily life is at hand: wood for houses, fruit and animals for food.

It is this world which lies behind the Sanema creation stories and way of life. At the beginning of the stories, the forest and some of its creatures and plants are already there. And these creatures show the threat and promise of the forest.

The Sanema's world and way of life show this fear and promise in many ways. Threat is shown by the vengeful ghosts of animals which have been killed. While the forest has food for the Sanema, it is not given so willingly when it comes to animals and birds. But if these vengeful ghosts do attack, say by making someone ill, then there are other even more powerful spirits who will help the Sanema. These are the hekula spirits of the different kinds of animals, birds and trees.

When the Sanema use trees to build their villages, there is no sense of threat. A village will probably have a number of families living in it. Each family builds a part of the village, side by side with the other families. So the people end up with a great, circular, thatched building, with a central courtyard open to the sky. The village is built of trees, vines and branches from the forest. A small area around it will be cut back to make a garden for growing yuca, yams, maize and other crops. There is no sense of the forest taking revenge on the people for doing this, because when they leave the village, the buildings simply rot back into the ground, and the forest grows back very quickly.

When it comes to hunting, then there is a sense of threat. To kill something is to take it away from the forest, from nature. When hunters from the village kill a creature, they believe they have released its ghost, and made it angry. It will probably seek revenge. So special rituals are performed by the shaman if the hunters, or anyone who has eaten the meat, falls ill. Meat is enjoyed, but the Sanema are very aware of what they have had to do to get that meat.

There is another Sanema belief which shows this using and being used by the forest. The people believe that when a baby boy is born, a

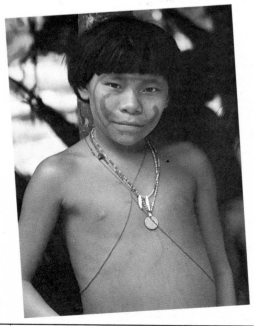

52

harpy eagle lays an egg at exactly the same time. This egg with its chick grows into an eagle, just as the boy grows into a man. If the boy or man becomes ill, then the chick or eagle becomes ill. If the eagle is injured, then the boy or man will be injured. When one dies, so does the other. They may never actually see one another, but they are part of each other.

For a girl, her 'partner' is a small creature like a weasel. Again, exactly the same things happen as between the boy and the eagle. So the Sanema do not kill harpy eagles or these weasel creatures, for they believe to do so would be to kill a human being.

Unfortunately, the balance which the Sanema have with the forest and its life is now under threat. Outsiders are coming to the forest. They are cutting down so many trees that the forest cannot recover. They are shooting so many animals that some species are dying out. All this has brought sickness, death and destruction to many of the forests' tribes. It may be that in a few years, this delicate balance of nature and people will have been destroyed beyond repair. If this is so, then the Sanema, those who fear, respect, use and care for the forest, will also disappear.

· Things to think about ·

The animals and trees around the Sanema are very special to them. The Sanema believe that they themselves were made from trees, and that their first teacher was a giant snake. What do you think you could learn from an animal or plant? Are there any animals or plants you feel close to? If so, which ones?

The Sanema feel that the forest can be dangerous and threatening, but it also gives food and things that they need. The Sanema try to balance the threat and promise of the forest. Do you think that you and the people around you still feel any fear or promise from nature?

The Sanema have been keeping the balance with the forest for a very long time, but now their way of life is in danger. The rain forests which have been there for so long are being destroyed by outsiders. Do you think this has to happen, or do you think people can find other ways of sharing the world?

· Word List ·

Aborigine   the first people to live in a particular land or island; the 'original' people.

Adam   a Hebrew word meaning 'man'.

altar   the special raised part of a church or temple where the most holy things are kept.

ancestors   people in your family or group who lived before you.

atman   a Sanskrit word usually translated as 'soul', but can also mean life, breath and movement.

belief system   a set of ideas or beliefs by which a person lives his or her life.

Bible   the Christian holy book, which is divided into two main parts. These are the Old Testament, which has the Jewish Torah in it, and the New Testament, which begins with the life of Jesus.

big bang   a name given to one idea about how the universe began. This idea says that the universe started with a huge explosion.

Buddhism   one of the great world religions. Buddhism began with a teacher called the Buddha in India around 550 BCE. 'Buddha' means the 'enlightened one'.

Call to Prayer   the call which tells Muslims to come to prayer. This call is made from the top of a mosque, from a tower called a minaret.

ceremonies   in religions, a ceremony is usually a set of actions which mark a special event, such as birth or marriage.

chaos   a state where nothing is organized or working together with anything else.

Confucianism   a set of rules for living, taught by K'ung Fu'tzu (Confucius) in China.

cursed   a curse is a wish that something bad will happen to someone or something. It is a very strong wish, and the person or object the wish is made about is said to be cursed.

cycle   a circle of events. This circle or cycle does not have a beginning or an end since, although it may seem to end, it then begins again.

dharma   this Sanskrit word can be said to mean 'duty'. A person's dharma is what he or she is supposed to do. People have different positions in life, and so have different duties.

disciples   the followers of a religious leader or teacher. The followers of Jesus were called disciples.

Dreamtime   the time when Australian Aborigines believe the world was created, but which still exists as life continues. Also called the **Dreaming**.

evil one   Muslims believe that this is a powerful being who fights against Allah (God), encouraging people to do things which are wrong.

Exodus   the time when the Jews left Egypt, where they were slaves, to find the land which God had promised them.

Fall, the   a name Christians use for the time when Adam and Eve ate the fruit they had been told not to eat, and were thrown out of the Garden of Eden.

festivals   special occasions. Religious festivals are times when the followers of a religion celebrate a day when something special happened, or think about an important person or idea in their religion.

forefathers   people in your family or group who lived before you; ancestors.

Garden of Eden   the place in the Christian creation story where the first man and woman lived until they disobeyed God.

goanna   a large Australian lizard.

God   a god is a very powerful being whom people worship and pray to. Many people believe there is only one God, and they talk about this being as God, using a capital 'G' to show they mean the one and only God.

harmony   a state where all things are balanced and work together properly.

Holy Communion   the Christian ceremony which remembers the Last Supper (Matthew 26:26-29). Christians share bread and wine as Jesus shared them with his disciples just before he died.

instinct   when people or creatures do things without thinking about them, they are said to be acting by instinct. For example, if you blink when something comes quickly towards your eyes, this is acting by instinct.

karma a Sanskrit word meaning 'work' or 'action'. In Indian belief, every action has results which affect the person who does the action. These results decide what the person will be reborn as.

lotus flower an Indian water-plant with large, pink flowers.

Mahatma this Sanskrit word means 'great soul', a title used to describe the Indian leader, Gandhi.

Mass see **Holy Communion.**

Messiah a Hebrew word meaning 'anointed one'; a promised leader to be sent by God.

monastery a place where followers of a religion can live and dedicate their time to prayer, meditation and worship.

mosque a Muslim place of worship, where Muslims can pray and learn about their religion.

mutations changes in living creatures, which make them different from their ancestors.

Nicene Creed a statement of Christian beliefs, drawn up by the Council of Nicaea in 325 CE.

Original ancestors creatures which the Yanomamo believe were the first ones of each kind of animal. All animals are believed to come from them.

Paradise another name for the Garden of Eden, used by Jews, Christians and Muslims.

Passover a Jewish festival which celebrates the Jews' escape from Egypt. The story of the Passover tells of how the angel of death came to the houses of the Egyptians, but passed over the houses of the Jews.

prophets messengers of God who tell people what God wants them to do.

rabbi a Hebrew word meaning 'teacher'. In a synagogue, the Jewish place of worship, the rabbi explains the Torah and leads the worship.

reborn to be reborn is to be born again in a new body.

religion a set of beliefs about a God or gods, which gives people a way in which to live their lives.

repentance this means being sorry for something you have done, and trying to do something about it, either by putting it right or by not doing it again.

rituals a special set of actions which have a religious meaning.

sacred something which is treated in a very special way because it has an important place in a religion, is said to be sacred.

saviour someone who saves or rescues people.

shaman a holy or special person in some tribal religions who is in charge of the religious rituals.

Shavuot a Jewish festival which was originally a spring harvest festival. Later it became a day when people remembered how Moses, a great Jewish leader, received the Ten Commandments.

sin doing wrong; doing what God does not wish you to do.

soul a part of a person which is believed not to die when that person's body dies.

Succot a Jewish festival also known as the festival of Booths, when booths or small huts are built of branches and decorated with leaves and fruit. It is a harvest festival, and also reminds Jews of the Exodus when they had to live in tents.

surah a division or chapter of the Qur'an, the Muslim holy book.

Supreme One in Hinduism, this is the being believed to be above every other being, and responsible for everything that exists.

symbol a sign, object or picture which stands for a particular idea or thing.

Talmud a Jewish book written by rabbis long ago to explain the ideas in the Jewish holy book, the Torah.

Taoism a set of Chinese beliefs, outlined in a book called the Tao Te Ching, said to have been given by Lao Tzu.

Torah the Jewish holy book.

tradition a story or idea handed down through the ages by word of mouth.

U

Upanishad a Sanskrit word meaning 'to sit down near', so called because these teachings were passed on to people who sat at their teachers' feet.

THE WORLD WILDLIFE FUND

What You Can Do

Many people are not careful about the way they treat the natural world. As a result the air we breathe is no longer clean and safe and the very soil we depend on for our crops is washed away by careless farming. Many animals and plants are threatened. The places where they live or grow are used or polluted by us and many animals are hunted to extinction. The dodo, for example, was an amazing flightless bird which was hunted for food by sailors and disappeared from the world in the seventeenth century. Gorillas, tigers and whales could all face the same fate if we do not decide that we wish them to live. Not only are all living things part of the world that we share, but they form part of the complicated links that support life on this planet.

The World Wildlife Fund tries to overcome these problems by raising money to protect forests, islands, marshes, meadows, the sea shores and the oceans from careless or irresponsible development. It also raises money so that people can find out more about the problems, and take action which will allow humans to live in greater harmony with nature. WWF also informs people about what is happening in our world so that they will want to make it a better place in which to live.

The problems are so vast that it may seem that we are unable to do anything about them, but if we all know and care about the world, that is an important first step.

However if you want to be more practically involved, there are a number of organizations which can give you help. For example, the Young Ornithologists Club and Watch can help you to learn more about wildlife in Britain, and both can give you practical advice on how you can make the place where you live a better place for wildlife. The British Trust for Conservation Volunteers organizes practical conservation activities and the World Wildlife Fund has a scheme designed to help groups of young people to become involved in improving the quality of their environment. It also has a Junior Membership section.

If you would like further details of these and other activities write to:

World Wildlife Fund
Panda House
11-13 Ockford Road
Godalming
Surrey GU7 1QU

56